ROVING THE RED PLANET

MISSION: MARS

T0062305

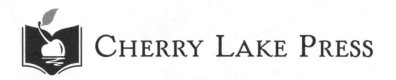

CHERRY LAKE PRESS

Published in the United States of America by Cherry Lake Publishing
Ann Arbor, Michigan
www.cherrylakepublishing.com

Reading Adviser: Beth Walker Gambro, MS, Ed., Reading Consultant, Yorkville, IL
Book Designer: Book Buddy Media
Photo Credits: Cover: ©NASA / nasa.gov; page 1: ©Anterovium / Shutterstock; page 5:
©NASA / Getty Images; page 7: ©NASA / nasa.gov; page 9: ©Natapong Supalertsophon /
Getty Images; page 10: ©NASA / Getty Images; page 13: ©NASA / nasa.gov; page 15: ©NASA/
JPL / nasa.gov; page 16: ©NASA/JPL-Caltech / nasa.gov; page 19: ©NASA / nasa.gov; page 21:
©Tony Gray/Nasa/ZUMAPRESS / Newscom; page 23: ©NASA/JPL-Caltech / nasa.gov; page
25: ©NASA / nasa.gov; page 27: ©NASA / nasa.gov; page 28: ©NASA/JPL-Caltech / nasa.gov;
page 29: ©onurdongel / Getty Images; page 30: ©NASA / nasa.gov

Copyright ©2022 by Cherry Lake Publishing Group
All rights reserved. No part of this book may be reproduced or utilized in any form or by any
means without written permission from the publisher.

Cherry Lake Press is an imprint of Cherry Lake Publishing Group.

Library of Congress Cataloging-in-Publication Data has been filed and is available
at catalog.loc.gov

Cherry Lake Publishing would like to acknowledge the work of the Partnership for
21st Century Learning, a Network of Battelle for Kids.
Please visit *http://www.battelleforkids.org/networks/p21* for more information.

Printed in the United States of America
Corporate Graphics

ABOUT THE AUTHOR

Mari Bolte is a children's book author and editor. Streaming sci-fi on TV is more her
speed but tracking our planet's progress across the sky is still exciting! She lives in
Minnesota with her husband, daughter, and a house full of (non-Martian) pets.

TABLE OF CONTENTS

CHAPTER 1

Destination: Mars

Thousands of years ago, the ancient Egyptians stared into the sky and charted the movements of the red planet they saw. It was not until 1965 that the idea of getting there was even possible. The first robotic explorer, the National Aeronautics and Space Administration's (NASA) rover *Sojourner*, touched down on the planet's surface in 1997. Since then, four more NASA rovers have landed: *Spirit*, *Opportunity*, *Curiosity*, and *Perseverance*. China is the only other country to have landed a rover. Theirs, called *Zhurong*, touched down in 2021.

Humans have not yet set foot on Mars. Until the planet is ready for us, scientists will learn everything they can with rovers.

Sojourner was launched on December 4, 1996. It landed on Mars on July 4, 1997. It sent more than 550 pictures back to Earth during its 83 days on the Red Planet.

Rovers are motor vehicles that travel across moons and planets in space. They collect samples, take pictures, and record the weather. Because they are machines, they can withstand the extreme temperatures on Mars. They do not need to eat or breathe, and they do not get tired. And they can carry a wide variety of tools as they explore.

Thanks to these robotic wheeled wonders, we have learned a lot about a planet that is 140 million miles (225 million kilometers) from Earth. With their help, humans may one day join them on the rocky surface of Mars.

The Mars Global Surveyor

The Mars Global **Surveyor** was launched on November 7, 1996. Its job was to **orbit** Mars for 2 years and map its surface. It began this work in March 1999 and performed this service until November 14, 2006.

The surveyor had a wide-angle camera lens that was used to take pictures of Mars every day. The pictures showed scientists repeating weather patterns, like dust storms that happened in the same location around the same time. It also used a laser altimeter. The altimeter sent laser pulses toward the planet's surface and recorded how long it took them to get there. It used that data to map **topographical** features, such as mountains or canyons.

Mars is full of challenges for a rover. The planet's surface is covered in broken rock. Mountains, canyons, **craters**, and **gullies** are additional obstacles a rover might have to roll over or around. Dust storms could blow a rover over, cause it to shut down, or even bury it.

People back on Earth control the rovers. Because the planets are so far apart, there is a delay between when the pilot gives a command and when the rover receives it. The same delay exists when it comes to the driver seeing what the rover sees. The delay is usually around 20 minutes. A lot can happen in this time! Because of this delay, each rover has a built-in navigation system. This navigation system helps the rover make its own

The *Mars Global Surveyor* stopped working in 2006, but the spacecraft is still in orbit around Mars.

decisions on how to get from point A to point B. But even then, the driver might not know what is happening until it has already happened.

Rovers move around the planet's surface on wheels. But they are not fast. They are only designed to roll around 328 feet (100 meters) a day. *Sojourner's* top speed was 0.015 miles (0.024 km) per hour. *Curiosity* and *Perseverance* traveled at 0.09 miles (0.14 km) per hour. *Spirit* and *Opportunity* were the fastest, at 0.1 miles (0.16 km) per hour. To compare, the average human walks between 3 and 4 miles (4.8 and 6.4 km) per hour!

Traveling Through Space

With the technology we have today, it takes at least 7 months to get to Mars. Spacecraft can only be launched every 26 months. During this window of time, Earth and Mars are as near as possible to each other. Researchers must figure out exactly how much energy it will take to get rovers from Earth to their landing site on Mars.

And it is a dangerous trip. On average, about half of all missions to Mars fail. Sometimes a part stops working. Sometimes the spacecraft do not survive the landing. Sometimes they land, but then lose communication with Earth.

[21ST CENTURY SKILLS LIBRARY]

NASA Mars Rovers

Ingenuity:
landed 2021; on
Perserverance;
4 pounds
(1.8 kg)

Curiosity:
landed 2012;
1,982 pounds
(899 kg)

***Spirit* and
*Opportunity:***
landed 2004; 384
pounds (174 kg)

Sojourner:
landed 1997 on
Pathfinder;
23 pounds
(10.4 kilograms)

Perseverance:
landed 2021;
2,260 pounds
(1,025 kg)

This diagram showing the evolution of Mars rovers is
etched onto a metal attached to *Perseverance*.

It took about 45 minutes for the spacecraft carrying *Curiosity* to separate from the rockets that sent it into space.

Rovers travel inside a spacecraft that protects them during the flight. To get past Earth's atmosphere, the spacecraft uses a launch vehicle. The launch vehicles look like long rockets. The spacecraft sits inside the cone-shaped top. The rest of the launch vehicle holds powerful rockets and their fuel. Fully assembled, the launch vehicle is 191 feet (58 m) tall and weighs around 1.17 million pounds (531,000 kg).

Running on the Sun

The first three rovers, Sojourner, Opportunity, and Spirit, used **solar power** *to run on electricity. Without the power of the Sun, they were not able to operate. The rovers had an* **array** *of solar panels. Opportunity and Spirit could collect around 140 watts of power a day. Those rovers need about 100 watts to run. This is equivalent to a light bulb in your house. Rechargeable batteries helped the rover operate on cloudy days or at night, but eventually the batteries wear out.*

Three stages of fuel burning get the rover into space. At each stage, a piece of the launch vehicle drops off, until just the spacecraft is left.

Finally, the rover is on its way to Mars! The spacecraft must keep its antenna pointed toward Earth and its solar panels pointed toward the Sun.

Rover Repair

*Because we can't send people to Mars yet, fixing equipment that malfunctions isn't always possible. In 2019, NASA's InSight lander needed help. Sent to explore the interior of Mars, it had a **probe** designed to drill 16 feet (4.9 m) into the soil. But the drill got stuck after just one foot (0.3 m). Scientists had no idea what to do. They couldn't take it out. The probe was not designed to be moved. It would stop working. So they just left it there until they could figure out a plan. In the end, they tried pressing the probe with InSight's arm. It worked!*

But, of course, hitting things to make them work is not an ideal solution! Mechanics and engineers on-site could solve problems as they happen. A rover repair shop would be a very helpful addition to the first Mars colony.

After flying through space for months, the rover's journey is almost over. When the spacecraft reaches Mars's atmosphere, it is going very, very fast—12,000 miles (19,320 km) per hour! That is almost 16 times the speed of sound back on Earth. A heat shield protects the spacecraft from burning up.

A parachute **deploys** to slow the spacecraft to around 200 miles (322 km) per hour. The heat shield falls off, revealing a sky crane. The crane is a hovercraft that uses **jet propulsion** to move. The rover is attached to its underside. The sky crane's jets fire immediately, slowing the descent even more. If all goes according to plan, the skycrane will hover around 20 feet

The SkyCrane was used to lower both *Curiosity* and *Perseverance* onto Mars's surface.

(6.1 m) above the planet's surface. It cannot land completely, because the jets could create a dust storm that would damage the rover. It lowers the rover onto the ground. Then it flies away so it does not crash into the rover.

NASA calls the entry, descent, and landing the "7 minutes of terror." That is how long it takes to land. But because of the communication delay between Earth and Mars, scientists on Earth have no idea how the landing is going. The spacecraft's computers must calculate the landing on its own. If even one thing does not work, the mission will fail.

CHAPTER 3

X Marks the Spot

Each rover sent to Mars has a specific mission. The goal of the *Mars Pathfinder*, with *Sojourner* in tow, was to show that scientists could send equipment to Mars without a high cost. *Sojourner* was the first wheeled vehicle used on any other planet in our solar system. It helped scientists understand what kinds of challenges future rovers would face.

Spirit and *Opportunity* were launched around the same time in 2003. They are also known as "the Adventure Twins." They were sent from different points on Earth, though, and had different landing spots on Mars. The rovers explored the planet's rocks and soils. They looked for signs of water, too. Meant to explore for 90 days, they both exceeded expectations. *Spirit* lasted for 6 years, 76 days. *Opportunity* spent 14 years exploring the planet.

[21ST CENTURY SKILLS LIBRARY]

Curiosity's Chemistry and Camera tool, also known as ChemCam, helped it identify chemicals and minerals in rocks and soil.

Curiosity was part of the Mars Science Laboratory mission. The rover was sent to explore the planet's **climate** and **geology**. Its job was to look for proof that **microbial** life ever existed on the planet. Any information gathered will be used to prepare humans for future exploration.

NASA's *Perseverance* rover fires up its descent stage engines as it nears the Martian surface.

The early rovers were looking for signs of microbial life. *Perseverance* was sent to look for proof of something bigger. What were the planet's surface and climate like in the past? Could it have supported a civilization? *Perseverance* also tested technologies that would help people use natural resources, which are natural substances found in nature. Water and minerals are natural resources.

Mars has very little oxygen. But if people are going to live on the planet, they will need to breathe! On April 23, 2021, *Perseverance* converted carbon dioxide from Mars's air into oxygen.

Built to Last

Rovers are not intended to work forever. Batteries and equipment only last so long. Just landing and gathering a little information is a huge accomplishment. Anything beyond that is an extra perk. Sojourner was only sent on a 1-week mission. The tiny rover rolled around for 83 days! Spirit surpassed its original 90 days by 25 times, operating for 6 years, 2 months, and 19 days. Opportunity was the longest-lived rover yet, staying active for 14 years, 136 days. Curiosity and Perseverance were sent on missions lasting 1 Mars year, or about 687 Earth days. Both are still active.

How have they lasted so long? For one thing, they are built of tough stuff. They are designed to handle Mars temperatures, which range from –220 to 70 degrees Fahrenheit (–140 to 21 degrees Celsius), depending on where you are on the planet. They also all have six wheels that carry the rover evenly. This makes it hard to tip them over. Their solar panels are designed to lean toward the Sun to collect solar energy.

The size of a small car, *Perseverance* is the largest rover to date. And it did not come alone. *Ingenuity* is a small, 4-pound (1.8 kg) drone helicopter that rode in on *Perseverance*. On April 19, 2021, *Ingenuity* proved that powered, controlled flight could be done on Mars.

CHAPTER 4

Exploring the Planet

Rovers have been finding proof that people could **colonize** Mars since *Opportunity* landed in 2004. The rover found minerals that need water to form. It found rocks that were shaped or moved by water. It found rocks full of clay that could not have been made without water.

Curiosity found elements like nitrogen, oxygen, and carbon that could create and support life. It also found methane. Methane is a gas that can be made by living things. What made the methane on Mars? No one knows—yet.

Perseverance carries advanced cameras, radar, and imaging tools.

Perseverance is equipped with a special ground-penetrating **radar**. Other expeditions have shown that there may be below-ground ice deposits. The radar is looking for them. The rover is also carrying five samples of space suit material. Scientists will see how each sample reacts to the **radiation** in Mars's atmosphere. Radiation is a form of energy that travels through space. Exposure to high levels of radiation can be deadly.

By the Numbers: Liftoff

Earth has 2.66 times more gravity than Mars. With things being lighter on the Red Planet, you would think that things would fly easier. However, the atmosphere on Earth is also denser. It is about 100 times denser than on Mars. On Earth, helicopter **rotor** *blades need to spin at 400 to 500 revolutions per minute (rpm) to lift off. On Mars, Ingenuity's rotors need to spin at 2,500 rpm. To duplicate that thinner atmosphere on Earth, a helicopter would have to fly at an altitude of 100,000 feet (30,480 m). This is around three times higher than airplanes usually fly. Luckily, scientists could use a* **vacuum chamber** *for their tests instead.*

Some people worry we might change Mars before we even get there. Around 30 spacecraft and landers have been sent to the Red Planet. Could any traces of Earth be left on any of them? Could microbes from Earth evolve to live in space? This idea is called forward contamination.

NASA has rules called protocols in place to prevent this. Rovers are built one layer at a time. Every piece is cleaned before it is added. Filters keep the air as pure as possible. But microbes are everywhere on Earth. It is hard to make something 100 percent clean. The danger is what might happen if those microbes do survive a trip to Mars. What if we find signs of life—but it turns out that life originated with us?

The *Atlas V* booster rocket sent *InSight*, *Curiosity*, and *Perseverance* into space. It cost $2.7 billion to get *Perseverance* to Mars.

Roving the Sea

The deepest place on Earth is in the Pacific Ocean between Japan and Indonesia. It is called Challenger Deep and it is 6.8 miles (11,000 m) under the sea. It is completely dark at the bottom and freezing cold. The water pressure could crush a human. What lives there has remained one of Earth's mysteries. Scientists hope that Perseverance's technology can uncover that mystery. A robotic vehicle called Orpheus was first tested in 2018. Both Perseverance and Orpheus use cameras to look around and identify nearby landmarks. In May 2021, Orpheus began a mission to map the ocean's floor. Eventually, it will tackle Challenger Deep. Scientists hope that someday a fleet of Orpheus-like robots could explore both the ocean and space.

In 1956, the first concerns about contaminating Mars were discussed. When the *Apollo 11* astronauts landed on the Moon in 1969, there were no rules about protecting the solar system. The first astronauts who visited the Moon left 96 bags of garbage behind. This included human waste and food trash. These bags contained more than 1,000 species of microbes that live in the human digestive system.

Orpheus is designed to be easy to reproduce and simple to use. It can also be deployed off of small ships.

Today, there are planetary protection policies designed to prevent further polluting the solar system. But we currently have no way to bring rovers, orbiters, and other equipment back to Earth. When rovers stop working, they are left where they fall. Is it **ethical** for us to just leave them there?

CHAPTER 5

The Future

Rovers would need to be much larger and faster to be helpful to humans. NASA's Artemis mission is working to get astronauts to the Moon by 2024. The last piloted mission to the Moon was in 1972. The Artemis team will test out space colonization technology there, with the expectation that their results will also work on Mars. One project is a pressurized rover that will serve as both home and lab for human colonists. They will be able to drive from place to place in regular clothing, then put on space suits when they need to get out and explore.

NASA is not the only organization trying to bring humans to Mars. In the 1950s, the United States and Russia became tense rivals to produce the most advanced technology and

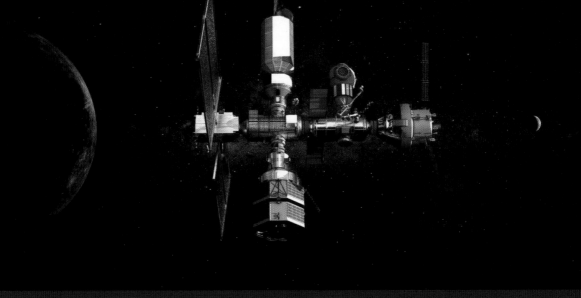

The *Gateway* outpost will be part of the Artemis mission to the Moon. It will orbit the Moon and serve as a docking location, delivery port, communication and control station, and life support system for Moon-landing crews.

weapons. This was called the Cold War. By the 1960s, the war to be first had extended into space. That period is called the Space Race.

Other countries have jumped into the Space Race, too. China landed its own rover on Mars in 2021. The United Kingdom Space Agency, China, the United Arab Emirates, and India have sent spacecraft to orbit Mars, too. In 2002, businessman Elon Musk founded SpaceX, a company whose goal is to send people to the Moon and to Mars. They have been sending cargo to the International Space Station (ISS) since 2012, and people since 2020, including 10 astronauts and four civilians.

Countries are already working together to conquer space. The ISS is operated by space programs in the United States, Europe, Russia, Japan, and Canada. As of April 2021, 243 people from 19 countries have visited the ISS.

Mars Road Trip

A huge dust storm stopped Opportunity *from collecting enough solar energy to run. The larger* Curiosity *and* Perseverance *rovers use plutonium for* **nuclear energy** *instead. The plutonium slowly decays, giving off heat that is converted to electric energy for the rover. A 10.6-pound (453.6 gram) piece of plutonium should power* Perseverance *for 14 years. That much plutonium isn't cheap, though. It costs around $4,000 per gram. That's quite a bit more than a tank of gas!*

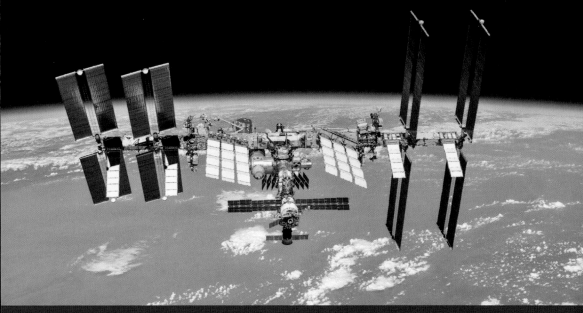

The ISS travels at 5 miles (8 km) per second. In 24 hours, the ISS orbits Earth 16 times.

But working together for science and colonizing new land are two different things. In 2020 and 2021, the United States and 11 other nations signed the Artemis Accords. This official agreement calls for nations to share data, register space objects, protect artifacts, and be peaceful toward each other. However, some countries think the accords should have been discussed and signed by every country. Russia and China, the two other countries with the most space advancement, did not sign it. What that means for the future of people on Mars is still unknown.

Ingenuity has made nine flights as of August 2021. Its longest flight covered 2,051 feet (625 m).

The success of *Ingenuity*'s flight opens the way to exploring the skies around Mars. Helicopters would give a sharper viewpoint of the planet than the orbiters in space. They can fly faster than rovers move. And, much like how soldiers on Earth use drones, they could also be useful tools for locating areas for future human missions.

Because of the thin atmosphere, it is unlikely that aircraft capable of carrying a human's full weight will work on Mars. But by increasing the helicopter rotors about three times the size of *Ingenuity*'s, they could carry heavy loads. Imagine receiving a package or your dinner by air on Mars! What else might be possible?

Growing food with reduced sunlight, oxygen, and water are all things farmers on Mars will have to think about.

Dining In

With people stuck at home during COVID-19, meal delivery services jumped in popularity. Colonists on Mars would be stuck at home for a different reason. Going out because you don't feel like cooking wouldn't be an option. And the dinner choices would be pretty limited! But you could share your food with other people. Maybe you could grow tomatoes and lettuce, and your neighbor could grow carrots and radishes. You could swap veggies and have a fresh, colorful salad without ever leaving your pressurized houses.

Activity: Message in Morse

A ·—   B —···   C —·—·   D —··   E ·

F ··—·   G ——·   H ····   I ··   J ·———

K —·—   L ·—··   M ——   N —·   O ———

P ·——·   Q ——·—   R ·—·   S ···   T —

U ··—   V ···—   W ·——   X —··—   Y —·——

MORSE   Z ——··   CODE

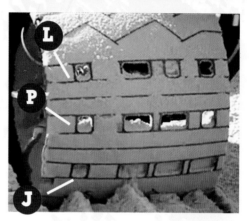

Morse code is a series of dots and dashes that represent letters and numbers. *Curiosity* contained a message in Morse code in its wheel treads. The dots and dashes it left in the soil spelled "JPL," short for Jet Propulsion Laboratory, which worked with NASA on the rover's mission. *Perseverance* carries a laser-etched plate with the message "Explore as One" hidden in Morse code. Learn Morse code and hide your own secret messages in your art.

WHAT YOU'LL NEED:

- **pencil and paper**
- **Morse code alphabet**

1. Think about the message you want to send. Write it out until it's a version you like.

2. Use the Morse code alphabet above to translate your message from the ABCs to dots and dashes.

3. Swap dashes with another person. Use the Morse code alphabet to translate the message back to the ABCs.

Find Out More

BOOKS

Loh-Hagan, Virginia. *Mars Colonization*. Ann Arbor, MI: Cherry Lake Publishing, 2020.

London, Martha. *Space Drones*. Minneapolis, MN: Abdo Publishing, a division of ABDO, 2021.

Lonely Planet Kids. *Future Worlds*. Oakland, CA: Lonely Planet, 2021.

Vago, Mike. *The Planets Are Very, Very, Very Far Away: A Journey Through the Amazing Scale of the Solar System*. New York, NY: The Experiment, 2021.

WEBSITES

BBC: Mars Rovers
https://www.bbc.co.uk/news/topics/cx099npv6v6t/mars-rovers
Meet the rovers currently on Mars, from *Zhurong* to *Perseverance*.

NASA's Mars Exploration Program
https://mars.nasa.gov/
The source of the latest Mars information, NASA's Exploration Program has all the most recent news about the Red Planet.

NISE Network: Exploring the Solar System: Mars Rovers
https://www.nisenet.org/catalog/exploring-solar-system-mars-rovers
Play a game to learn about how rovers are used to explore distant lands.

The Planetary Society: Every Mission to Mars, Ever
https://www.planetary.org/space-missions/every-mars-mission
Who has landed on Mars? Where did the rovers land? Which are still active? And what's in store for the future?

GLOSSARY

array (uh-RAY) an arrangement

climate (KLY-muht) the weather conditions in an area over a long period of time

colonize (KOL-uh-nyz) to send a group of settlers to a new place

craters (CRAY-tuhrz) large bowl-shaped depressions in the ground

deploys (duh-PLOYZ) moves something into position

ethical (ETH-uh-kuhl) an action or behavior that is right or good

geology (gee-AH-luh-gee) the makeup and physical features of an area

gullies (GUH-leez) deep cuts made in the ground, usually by moving water

jet propulsion (JET pro-PUL-shuhn) an object's movement by high-speed jets of gas or liquid

microbial (my-KROW-bee-uhl) the presence of very small living things, called microbes; microbes include bacteria, algae, and amoebas

nuclear energy (NOO-klee-ur EHN-ur-jee) energy created by splitting tiny particles of matter

orbit (OR-bit) the curved path of an object in space around a star, planet, or moon

probe (PROHB) an unpiloted spacecraft that travels through space to collect information

radar (RAY-dahr) a system for detecting objects by sending out pulses or waves; the waves are reflected off the object and back to the source

radiation (ray-dee-AY-shuhn) a form of energy that travels through space

rotor (RO-tuhr) a hub with a number of arms that is rotated to provide lift to a helicopter or drone

solar power (SOH-luhr POW-uhr) power gained by harnessing the energy of the Sun's rays

surveyor (sur-VAY-uhr) a spacecraft used to examine or record an area of land on Mars

topographical (top-uh-GRA-fik-uhl) relating to the arrangement of the physical features of an area

vacuum chamber (VAK-yoom CHAYM-buhr) a container where air and other gases are removed to create a low-pressure environment inside the chamber known as a vacuum

INDEX